HOW TO WALK WITH GOD

HOW TO WALK WITH GOD

(formerly
What Now)

David Winter

Scripture Union
47 Marylebone Lane, London W1M 6AX

First published 1969 under the title What Now
First published in this edition in the UK 1977 by Scripture Union,
47 Marylebone Lane, London WIM 6AX

ISBN 0 85421 543 3
Photoset and printed in Malta by Interprint (Malta) Ltd.

Contents

Introduction

Barbara threw her arms around me at the church door. Her smile was dazzling and it was obvious that she had to overflow to someone. It happened to be me.

'Oh, isn't being a Christian *great*? During the service this morning I felt lifted right out of myself! And all week long it's as if I've been talking with Jesus face-to-face! He's been making the most fantastic things happen! I just want to shout "Praise the Lord" all the time, don't you?'

'Yeah.' I disentangled myself and smiled wanly, lying through my teeth. 'Fabulous,' I muttered. 'Just fabulous.'

I diverted my eyes from her glowing face and tried to figure out where the kids had got to, who had parked his car across the front of mine, and how I could possibly explain that I couldn't make the action study group on Tuesday, after all. As I walked to the car I was suddenly and painfully aware that Barbara was one sort of Christian and I was another.

And this book is for both kinds: the ones who find the Christian life 'just one miracle after another' and those who feel bogged down in their own discouragement; both those who get caught up to the seventh heaven during Sunday morning worship and those whose emotional response is *nil*; for those who feel the close, warm presence of God when they pray as well as those who can almost *hear* all their prayers bouncing back from the ceiling.

'Just as you trusted Christ to save you,' writes Paul in his letter to the Colossians[1], 'trust him, too, for each day's problems; live in vital union with him.' The King James version puts the same verse this way: 'As ye received Christ Jesus the Lord, so *walk* ye in him.'

I like that word 'walk.' A walk is the most natural, steady, unsensational way of getting from one place to another. Barbara may seem to hop, skip and jump her joyful way to heaven. But living in the clouds, she may miss some of the realities of life. She doesn't need a book to help her to enjoy worship. What she needs is help in living consistently for Christ, in learning to be steady and responsible, in growing in love and understanding of those whose experience with God seems less exuberant than hers. She needs to learn to *walk*.

People like me need a different kind of help. We need to know how to keep up the pace of our walk with God without getting defeated and discouraged. We need help with the whole idea of prayer, and of faith. We need joy that doesn't depend on lots of 'fantastic things happening.' We are children of God just as surely as Barbara is. And we need to learn to *walk*, too.

To walk with somebody you have to observe three simple ground rules. First you must meet somewhere before you start. Next, you must agree about where you are going. And then, you both have to walk at the same speed.

The same rules apply to our walk with God. We have to agree to meet somewhere—and that 'meeting place' has already been decided on. We must meet God at the cross, where Jesus died. That may sound rather mystical and abstract, but it really makes sense. What keeps us away from God is sin. That's why we must come back to him at the place where sin was dealt with—at the cross, where Jesus died for our sins. When we are truly sorry for all our wrongdoing, and confess it, and turn from it, and believe with all our hearts that Jesus died to free us from wrongdoing, past and future, and put ourselves under his command for life—it is then *we meet God.* That's when 'the walk' can begin. But it's futile to try to walk with God if you have not yet met him at the appointed place.

Then, we have to agree about where we are going—and where we are going is eternity, life with God, heaven. 'You know where I am going,' Jesus told his disciples.[2]

'No, we don't,' Thomas said. 'We haven't any idea where you are going!'

So then Jesus made it perfectly clear to them—'No one can *get to the Father* except by means of me,' he said. So 'getting to the Father' is our goal, our destination; not 'being happy,' or 'doing good,' or 'pleasing our parents' (though these may be by-products). We cannot walk with God unless and until we know where we are going. When we are clear about the destination, we can start walking.

And when we do, we must walk at our companion's pace. If you go for a walk with, say, the Duke of Edinburgh, you do not dash ahead, leaving him to trail behind. Nor do you hang back, chatting with the bystanders, or window-shopping. When we are walking with someone we respect, or love, we adjust our pace to theirs, heading together toward an agreed destination.

That is a rather good picture of our Christian life—walking with God. It is not a breathless sprint to heaven, nor a reluctant crawl. It is steady, regular, disciplined progress in the company of a Friend.

A tourist friend of mine asked an Arab the way to his local market. The Arab nodded politely and said, 'I am the way,' and walked with my friend to the market. It was his way of saying, 'I'll go with you.'

As we walk with God, Jesus says to us, 'I am the way.' And it is simply an offer to go with us. We walk with God the Son—to God the Father. That is what this book is all about.

[1]*Colossians 2.6* (The Living Bible)

[2]*John 14.4, 5, 6* (The Living Bible)

The following chapters have been written to provide you with certain basic information about walking with God by living the Christian life. At the end of each chapter there is a self-check test which you may use to reinforce your grasp of the chapter content.

Answers to self-check test questions may be found on page 96.

1
WHAT *IS* A CHRISTIAN?

So you've 'become a Christian?' Good. Naturally you want to get on as quickly as possible with the business of *being* a Christian, which is what this book is really about. But I'm sure you won't object if we spend the first chapter trying to answer one very important question—because if you get this answer wrong, things are sure to fall apart sooner or later.

What is a Christian?

The only logical way to start a book on 'living the Christian life' is to define what we mean by 'Christian.' Otherwise we may be talking at cross-purposes from beginning to end. After all, 'Christian' is one of the most widely used and mis-used words in the language. An opinion poll taken in broad daylight in the suburb of a large city produced such varied definitions as these:

A white man
A Protestant
A Roman Catholic
Someone who is kind and thoughtful

A member of a church
Someone who believes in God
A person who does his best
A religious person
A follower of Jesus Christ

Obviously some of these answers are better than others, but none of them is the whole truth (the last one gets closest to it) and some of them are totally misleading. If people in an historically 'Christian' country—there's that word again—are so confused about its meaning, it is necessary to pin down exactly what a Christian *is* right at the start of this book.

The simplest statement is that a Christian is one who believes in and walks with Jesus Christ. But that means something only if we know who Jesus Christ is. Unfortunately, we hardly ever start far enough back in these definitions. Many misunderstandings about Christianity, and many failures and problems within it, stem from a faulty grasp of basic elements of the faith.

There are three fundamental truths in the Christian faith, and they are all touched on in a verse in one of Paul's letters—I Timothy 2.5: 'For there is one God, and there is one mediator between God and men, the man Christ Jesus.'

There is One God

Most people believe in 'God,' but they don't know what he is like. They think of him as someone up in the sky who manipulates men and materials like a man controlling puppets on a string. Or else they think he is a kind father-figure, waiting in the wings of life to be called on stage when tragedy, disaster or danger threatens, to rescue us and make everything better again. Or they may imagine a stern judge, sipping a lengthy cup of coffee and waiting for the final speeches before stepping back into court and rewarding the good and punishing the bad. Even Christians can be found holding these inadequate views of God, and experiencing all kinds of confusion and doubt as a result.

God is infinite

The Christian God (we should best call him the 'God of the Bible') is first of all *infinite*. When he was dedicating the great Temple in Jerusalem, King Solomon prayed to God and said: 'Behold, heaven and the highest heaven cannot contain thee.'[1] That is a profound truth. God is not limited, as we are, by time or space. His existence had no beginning, and it will never end. His very name, Jehovah (more correctly *Yahweh*) simply means 'I AM'—in other words, he is permanently present tense.

I *was* born; I *am* alive; I *shall* die. That is human chronology. But God permanently and eternally *is*. That is why the question, 'But who made God?' has no meaning—and no answer, because anything 'made' could not possibly be 'God' at all.

God is infinite, without beginning or ending, and it's impossible to think of him in our space-time terms. Space exploration, astronomy, physics and so on can tell us nothing about a God who, as the Bible teaches, is an infinite Spirit not to be thought of as being 'somewhere' (the only answer to the question 'Where is God?' is 'everywhere') nor tied to time. God is not 'dead' because God was never 'born': he is just alive, or—more accurately—he just *exists*.

God is personal

The Christian God, secondly, is *personal.* He is not simply a vague Force or Power in the universe, nor an almighty dynamo or computer sparking off energy or knowledge in all directions, but a Person, with all the attributes of personality.

This is not to say, of course, that he is a man, or even a superman. God has no body, no arms or legs or face or eyes. Jesus said 'God is Spirit.'[2] The Psalmist said, 'Whither shall I flee from thy presence?'[3] If God is present everywhere he cannot be confined to a 'body,' as we are.

The most convincing argument that God is personal is the human race, for if God's most advanced creatures are persons it would seem to follow that he cannot be less than personal himself.

God is good

The third attribute of God which is vitally important in understanding Christianity is that he is *good.* This may seem obvious, but, in fact, there have always been people, and there are today, who believe that there *is* a God, but that he is either morally bad, or morally neutral. The former view expresses itself in black magic (in its extremer forms), and the latter in the very common belief that God, having made the world and mankind, cares nothing about our fate and is merely a spectator of events.

When the Christian says that God is good he is making a profound statement. He is saying that the one who created the universe, and all things in it, is not neutral in the ceaseless war between good and evil but is deeply involved in it. We'll discuss later on how it is possible for a good God to be the Creator of a world containing so much that is evil, and also the chief ground upon which Christians argue that he is good.

God is good not comparatively, as humans are, but absolutely. When I say 'so-and-so is good,' I really mean he is as good as I am, but certainly not perfect. But when I say 'God is good' I mean that he is absolutely and utterly good, with a blazing purity of both motive and action which human beings cannot possibly grasp. 'God is light and in him is *no darkness at all*,' claims John.[4] The Bible's most common adjective to describe God is, simply, 'holy.'

So Christians believe, and the Bible teaches, that God is infinite, personal and good. To grasp what that statement means is to take an immense step forward as a human being. To fail to grasp it is to leave in your thinking the seeds of wrong ideas which may lead to problems in matters of faith and of daily Christian living.

'There is one God,' Paul told Timothy. But he went on, in the verse we quoted earlier, to mention two other identities—'men,' and 'the man Christ Jesus.'

Human beings

'Men,' or human beings, are made in the 'image of God.'[5] This, again, is a profound statement, made in the opening chapter of the Bible. To have been made in the 'image of God' does not, and, as we have seen, cannot mean that we 'look like' God. Even less does it mean that God looks like us, as some people have supposed. It means that man shares some of God's characteristics, especially personality and morality. That is to say, human beings are persons, not animals: able to love, think in terms of ideas, enjoy art and music, express themselves and (to some extent) control their environment; and they are moral beings, having consciences and being able to make moral distinctions. Part of being a human is this instinct about right and wrong, however crude the concept or however warped it has become since the creation. To be made in the 'image of God' means that man is *significant*, he really matters. God loves mankind and cares for each member of the human race.

But the Bible also teaches that man, while significant, is also lost. He has run his life contrary to God's will and organized his society without reference to its Maker: and the results have been disastrous. God is not to be blamed for the present state of the world. He made it 'very good.'[6] But inherent in being a human is the fearful right to decide in moral matters, and man has used that right all down history to disobey God and disregard the Maker's instructions. The price to be paid for his sin and failure is all around us, in crime, disease, disillusionment and war.

It is also to be seen in man's 'lostness.' All down the ages men have written and sung about their sense of need, of the apparent futility of life, of its shortness and its sad sweetness. Human beings, as a race, are a strange people, restless and unsatisfied. How can it be otherwise, when through the 'Fall' they have lost true knowledge of their Creator, who alone gives direction, meaning and motive for life?

So the Bible teaches that man is significant, but lost.

Jesus Christ

'The man Christ Jesus,' however—to use Paul's unique

description of Christ—is a different calibre of 'man' altogether. Jesus Christ is God's sole and complete answer to the human dilemma. God is infinite, personal and perfect. Man is finite, personal and imperfect. Between them yawns a chasm as wide as eternity, between the blazing purity of the Creator and the rebellion and squalid sin of his creatures.

'The man Christ Jesus' is God's answer. Paul describes him as a 'mediator'—that is, a go-between. The perfect mediator is someone who can perfectly represent each opposing party to the other. The ideal industrial mediator, for instance, would be a man who had worked in industry both on the shop floor and also in management. Jesus Christ is the perfect mediator between God and men because he shares both natures. As the eternal Son, he is divine. As Jesus of Nazareth, a flesh-and-blood man of the first century, he is human. Alone of all men who have ever lived, he can stand between the Father and his rebel creatures as a true mediator.

In the following verse of I Timothy, Paul explains how Christ can bring us to God. He is the one 'who gave himself as a ransom for all.' A ransom is a price paid for the freedom of a prisoner, and it was that price which Jesus Christ paid when he died for us. He lived on earth a perfect life: perfect alike in motive and action. He 'went about doing good,' and giving outstanding moral instruction, too. Even his judge had to admit that he could 'find no fault in him.'[7] And then he took that perfect human life—the only perfect one ever lived on earth—and offered it as a sacrifice for the sins of all the other human beings who had lived, were living or were yet to live upon this planet. God accepted this sacrifice, confirmed it by raising Jesus from the dead, and now offers forgiveness and new life to all who turn from sin and receive his Son by faith.

Jesus Christ claimed to be the Son of God.[8] He proved the claim by the sort of life he lived. At the same time, he proved beyond dispute the goodness of God. He did this in his own life and actions, and because 'in this the love of God was made manifest among us, that God sent his only Son into the world, so that we might live through him.'[9] Baptism represents this.

To recapitulate: God is infinite, personal and perfect; man is finite, personal and sinful. This means that man, though significant, is lost and cut off from God. Man therefore needs a mediator, or saviour, to bring him back to God, and God's own Son Jesus Christ is precisely the mediator and saviour we need. Those who turn from sin and receive Jesus Christ by faith are forgiven their sins, and given a new, spiritual life, which the Bible calls 'eternal life.'

This book is written for those who, through this tremendous experience—which Jesus Christ himself compared to being 'born again'[10]—have entered upon the Christian life. Only those who have come this way have a hope of living that life, for it is obvious that without birth there cannot be life. Many people down the ages have tried to live the Christian life without the 'new birth,' but the attempt has only led to despair and disillusionment. With all the help God gives his new-born children through the Holy Spirit, it is hard enough, as many a battle-scarred veteran of the 'fight of faith' will agree. Without his resources, walking with God is utterly impossible. In the next chapters we shall be seeing what those resources are, but the immediate question is whether they are ours, or whether we are trying to be do-it-yourself disciples. Those who have faced the facts about God's holiness and man's sin will not be under any illusion that they can somehow sprint through the gates of heaven to the Almighty on their own terms or in their own strength. It is at the start of the Christian life that we need to get these things straight, and then we shall find that for every need God has provided a complete answer. We shall have a healthy awareness of our own inability. We shall have a deep appreciation of the 'grace'—undeserved kindness—of a God who 'so loved the world that he gave his only Son, that whoever believes in him should not perish but have eternal life.' We shall not underestimate the difficulties involved in walking the path of Christianity in the modern world, but neither shall we underestimate the enormous power God makes available to his children, a power which is sufficient for their every need.

[1] *I Kings 8.27*
[2] *John 4.24*
[3] *Psalm 139.7*
[4] *I John 1.5*
[5] *Genesis 1.27*
[6] *Genesis 1.31*
[7] *Luke 23.4*
[8] *Mark 14.61, 62*
[9] *I John 4.9*
[10] *John 3.3*
[11] *John 3.16*

SELF-CHECK TEST 1

Circle the letter of the correct answer for each of the following. Choose the answer which most completely expresses the truth taught in the chapter.

1. Chapter one is most adequately summed up by the statement:
a. The fall of man has resulted in a lost human race which desperately needs a Saviour.
b. God has provided for lost mankind a personal and adequate Saviour and mediator in the person of the Lord Jesus.
c. The only mediator, Christ, is infinite, personal and good.
d. Man cannot be saved by his own efforts because his every attempt to do so leads to further frustration.

2. A Christian may adequately be described as
a. a good person.
b. a sincerely religious person.
c. a church member.
d. none of the above.

3. This chapter is based on
a. John 3.16
b. Acts 4.20
c. Romans 10.9
d. 1 Timothy 2.5

4. The attributes of God discussed in this chapter are these—God is:
a. infinite, personal and good.
b. omnipotent, omnipresent and omniscient.
c. loving, holy and righteous.
d. Creator, Redeemer and Sustainer.

5. The goodness of God is:
a. comparative, since God does not treat all people alike.
b. absolute, since he is holy.
c. comparative, since he allows evil to exist.
d. absolute, since he is neutral in the war between good and evil.

6. When the Bible says that man is made 'in the image of God' it means that
a. man looks like God.
b. God looks like man.
c. man shares some of God's characteristics.
d. images of God are helpful in worship.

7. Crime, disease and war together with human restlessness and a sense of futility prove that
a. man has lost his true knowledge of the Creator.
b. man has ceased to be significant to God.
c. man could not have been created by a loving God.
d. man was not created as a perfect being.

8. The ransom price Jesus paid in order to set sinners free was
a. his wealth, since he was rich, yet for our sakes became poor.
b. his perfect life, which he offered up as a sacrifice.
c. his character, which evil men slandered when they hired false witnesses against him.
d. his family, since it is written of him 'lover and friend hast thou put far from me.'

9. When a person becomes a Christian
a. God places infinite resources at his disposal to enable him to live the Christian life.
b. he is expected never to sin again.
c. he must go on in his own strength conscientiously seeking to be like Jesus.
d. he will never again be tempted.

2
WHAT HELP WILL GOD GIVE ME?

So it's difficult being a Christian . . . but God has given us some resources to help us walk with him. That's good news, because you may have already realized that you couldn't possibly keep it up on your own. In these next few chapters we'll talk about these resources—the really big and important things God has provided to help you and me to live the Christian life in a world like ours.

These resources are sometimes called the 'means of grace,' which simply expresses the same idea in a shorter phrase. However, people often think of them as isolated aids—rather like gadgets in a modern home to make the housewife's life easier—whereas they are really built-in elements of the Christian walk, more like lungs, heart and arteries in the human body, conveying blood exactly where it is needed.

They are the 'means of grace,' but not the grace itself. They are pipes through which water flows, but not the liquid itself. They are wires along which messages flow, but they are not the messages themselves. It is important to understand that.

People make lists of the various means of grace, and none will be complete, because God can use almost anything a Christian does to help and strengthen him. Making a bed, typing an invoice, brewing a pot of coffee could, in certain circumstances, be 'means of grace.' But the most common means, and the ones we shall deal with in this and the following chapters, are Christian fellowship, Bible reading, prayer, holy communion and service.

Christian fellowship

Some readers will be surprised that I have put this one first, even before the Bible. But it seems to me essential to be realistic. If we are 'born again' as Christians, then surely we are born into a family? The first help most of the Christians in the New Testament got after their conversion was not from the Bible, but from other Christians. For most of us, the vital encouragement in the early days and weeks of faith is the support, love and fellowship of Christian people—and in practice that means the Church.

Now there are dangers in saying this, and they ought to be mentioned at once. The most important of them is that the love and friendship of other Christians may distract us from the primary relationship, newly established, with God himself. We may blow hot on the creatures and go cold on the Creator. People can help us, but they are no substitute for God, and our fellowship with him.

The other aspect of this danger is that we may come to rely on other Christians too much. We may accept too naively all they tell us, without (like the Beroeans in the Bible[1]) checking what they tell us with the Scripture. Or they may become a crutch to a weak and immature walk of faith, propping us up by their presence and support, but disguising from us our true need to build 'upon the foundation of Jesus Christ.'[2] If we move to a new community, or go away to college or to hospital, we may find that our crutch has been suddenly removed, and our faith is revealed as the weak, second-hand thing it has become.

But, dangers apart, Christian fellowship is a wonderful aid on the Christian's path to heaven. It should be experienced in two directions: companionship with God, and companionship with other Christians.

The relationship with God comes first. If Jesus Christ died to mediate between God and men, then a line of communication has been opened between earth and heaven for all who are 'in Christ.' The New Testament is full of invitations to us to enter fellowship with God the Father, tell him our needs and draw upon his strength and comfort. This is not just a matter of 'prayer' in the technical sense (though we shall be discussing that later), but of a life lived in constant contact with God, open before him. This is the normal Christian life, though many of us through sin or negligence have let the lines of communication get rusty.

Fellowship with God is through Jesus Christ, and the Christian experience is often simply called 'knowing Christ.' Those who are Christians are frequently described in the New Testament as being 'in Christ'—and you can't have closer fellowship than that!

Probably the most vivid expression of this two-way relationship between God and the Christian, and between Christian and Christian, is the Lord's Supper, or 'holy communion.' Although Jesus Christ personally commanded us to observe it, and its first celebration on the evening of his betrayal is described in some detail in three of the four Gospels, many Christians admit that they feel they ought to 'get more' from it than they do.

The Lord's Supper should help us to understand our relationship with God, and with each other. Jesus Christ said that the bread and wine, broken and poured out in his Name, are his 'body and blood.' That is, they represent his death for us on the cross. If we look at them, we can remember what he did, and be thankful, but if we take and eat them, we are making what he did then part of us now—becoming personally involved. In fact, we were *not* told to admire the bread and wine, but to consume them. Similarly, we are not called simply to admire Jesus Christ, but to 'take him for ourselves,' to receive him and nourish our lives on his strength and goodness.

But this unique 'meal' is not eaten alone, as a solitary act of devotion. We come *with the family of God*, and share it with them. We sit around the table with others who have been saved in the same way, and depend upon the same Saviour for life and strength. Here, all are (or should be) equal, for both the needs and the standing of each are the same. Worship, at this level, really is the expression of a relationship of dependence, total and complete, upon what God has done for us in his Son.

Holy communion will only mean important things to us when we have grasped all this. It is a *family* meal, which pictures our unity and fellowship in Jesus Christ and it is a *real* meal, in which our spiritual life is nourished inwardly by Christ just as our physical life is nourished by the material elements of bread and wine.

Jesus Christ draws near to us as we draw near to

him. Those who come *expecting* to meet him, loving God and their fellow-Christians, will find they are not disappointed.

Preparation has a part in this. Confession of known sins, especially sins against our fellow-Christians; prayer that we may meet with Christ; study of passages of the Bible that tell of the sort of person Christ is and the sort of things he did on earth: these are ways to make sure that we do not miss the heart of what God has for us in this 'means of grace.'

The Christian is not expected to be praying—consciously, out loud—all day long. But he *is* told to 'pray constantly'[3]— to be constantly 'in an attitude of prayer.' Unbroken fellowship with God is the birth-right of the Christian. That companionship can be blurred, marred and even broken completely by sin, but once the sin is identified, repented of, confessed and cleansed by Christ, the relationship is restored as good as new.[4] This relationship with God—this fellowship—lies behind every means of grace. Without it, 'means' become mechanical and meaningless, a sort of empty shell without content or power. But the 'means of grace' themselves will help to build up and develop that relationship.

A couple who are not in love can kiss and embrace and call each other 'darling' (especially in front of friends), but these are empty gestures without a warm human relationship to give them meaning. But for a couple deeply in love, exactly the same embraces and words are 'means of grace,' not only expressing a true love for each other, but at the same time strengthening and deepening that love.

So it is with God and the Christian. The 'means of

grace' can be cold, mechanical exercises, without the living relationship. Or, with it, they may be expressions of his love for us, and ours for him. And they will also serve to deepen and enrich the loving, living relationship.

Fellowship with other Christians is simply an extension of our fellowship with God—and never the other way round. We are drawn to what there is of Christ in them, and 'deep calls to deep'. We love them in Christ and for his sake. That is not to say that our love for our fellow-Christians is *less* than human. But it may be *more* than human. Neither is it to say that we simply love them to please Christ, or because he commands it. Such 'love' wouldn't be genuine at all. To love for Christ's sake is simply to love in the way that Christ loves us, not because we deserve it, not because we are lovable, but because he is love. Our love for each other is a sort of overflowing of his love for us.

This may all sound rather mystical, but it is in fact vital, practical Christianity. If you hold back from this experience (loving God, loving each other) then you will end up an embittered, dried-up Christian, the light and joy gone from your religion, a dehydrated disciple. Jesus said that he was a well of living water, bubbling up in the believer, and that Christians would experience this same inner source of life flowing out into the lives of others.[5] Fellowship is not a luxury, not a decoration on top of Christianity. In a very real sense it *is* Christianity, for 'abiding in Christ' and 'loving each other' is what it's all about.[6]

But isn't 'church' boring?

Of course, to talk about 'fellowship' in this way is rather vague, but I've been trying to avoid using the word 'church' as far as possible, simply because it has such unfortunate connections in the minds of many people. Christian fellowship *is* the Church, in fact, and the Church *is* a fellowship of Christians. Unhappily, we find it hard to dissociate the *word* 'church' from buildings, services and meetings, but it is hardly ever used in this sense in the Bible.

'Church' means 'gathering' or 'assembly'—people coming together for the same reasons. Sometimes Christians 'come together' for worship ('services'), sometimes for study, sometimes for prayer, sometimes for common action; each of these is an occasion of Christian 'fellowship.'

Now, obviously, churches vary. In some there seems to be very little sense of fellowship; in others it is very strong. Rather than simply criticize your church if it seems to be lacking in warm fellowship, why not set out deliberately to create it—perhaps by being particularly friendly to fellow church members who live near you, by inviting people round for coffee after services, by visiting elderly members and so on? Fellowship cannot be organized, but it can be created and encouraged.

[1] *Acts 17.10, 11*
[2] *I Cor. 3.11*
[3] *I Thess. 5.17*
[4] *I John 1.9*
[5] *John 4.14*
[6] *John 15.4, 12*

SELF-CHECK TEST 2

Circle the letter of the correct answer for each of the following. Choose the answer which most completely expresses the truth taught in the chapter.

1. By 'means of grace' is meant
a. the grace that God gives to enable us to live the Christian life.
b. isolated aids ('gadgets') which smooth the Christian path.
c. built-in resources which make possible for the Christian a life pleasing to God.
d. the means by which a Christian attains sinless perfection in this life.

2. The practical focal point of Christian fellowship is
a. the church.
b. the home.
c. the home meeting.
d. the church service.

3. One of the dangers of Christian fellowship is that it
a. is a substitute for fellowship with God.
b. may become a crutch.
c. weakens our faith so that we can't stand for God without it.
d. may take up too much of our time.

4. The believer, in his special relationship with God, is described in the New Testament as being
a. 'in the world but not of the world.'
b. 'in fellowship.'
c. 'in Christ.'
d. 'in the ark.'

5. The Lord's Supper was instituted
a. by three of the four Gospel writers.
b. by Paul.
c. by the Church.
d. by the Lord Jesus.

6. The elements of which we partake in the Lord's Supper represent
a. our death with Christ.
b. Christ's death for us.
c. both of the above.
d. neither of the above.

7. The Lord's Supper is to be partaken of
a. as a means of salvation.
b. in fellowship with other believers.
c. as a religious obligation.
d. in solitude and private meditation.

8. Before partaking of the Lord's Supper we should
a. confess our sins.
b. examine our own hearts.
c. fast.
d. attend a preparatory church service.

9. Fellowship with God
a. can never be lost since it is the birthright of every Christian.
b. can be impaired and even broken by sin.
c. can never be regained once it is lost.
d. can never be attained in this life since it is one of the elements of the life to come.

10. Fellowship with other Christians
a. is motivated by a lesser type of love than that which we have for our blood relations.
b. is an extension of the natural love we have for other people.
c. is something we extend to them because they deserve it.
d. is an overflowing to other Christians of the love of God for us.

3
WHAT ABOUT THE BIBLE?

If God's means of help to us depend on a close walk—a relationship between God and ourselves, we had better ask in what ways we can communicate with him and he with us.

A husband and wife can speak to each other, listen to each other, touch each other and in a hundred other subtle human ways give expression to their love. Communication is vital to any real relationship, and that includes a relationship between God and men—it is not just a vague feeling, but a genuine person-to-person encounter. This means that we should expect to hear God speaking to us, and that we can, in some way, reply. To put it another way, we look for a genuine *dialogue* between our Father and his family.

The primary means by which God speaks to us is the Bible. The primary means by which we speak to him is prayer.

The Bible, in other words, is not just another book. We are not in a position to judge it or criticize it. It is the 'Word (or *expression*) of God', his own special revelation of truth about himself, about life and meaning.

This needs some explanation and justification. We have already said that we should expect to hear God speaking to us. In a sense this expectation flows from belief in the existence of a personal and good God.

Here we are in a vast universe, tiny specks of matter on an insignificant planet. We do not know where we have come from. We cannot explain why we are here. We do not know whether we have any destiny beyond the seventy or so short years of our lives. Night falls. Pain comes. Mysteries surround us. Dreams haunt our nights. Anxieties dog our days.

Now assume that there is, as Christians believe, an infinite, personal, good God who made us and the whole universe. He is our creator, and we are his creatures, baffled and more than a bit frightened by this strange world in which he has put us. If he does not wish to speak with us, to explain things to us and comfort us, *then he is not good.* If he is not able to communicate with us, *he is not personal*—for a basic element in being a 'person' is the ability to communicate with other persons. And if it is beyond his powers to communicate to all of us at once *he is not infinite*. God's very nature, in other words, demands that at some time, in some way, he must speak to us, and communicate some much-needed truth to us about ourselves, our existence, the nature of the universe in which he has set us, and our relationship to him.

Has God spoken like this? Christians believe that he has, and that the Bible is the record of his own special revelation to men. Within its pages he has explained all that we need to know on earth about himself, life, death, behaviour, time, eternity and ultimate purpose. It is called—and calls itself—the 'Word' of God, and that is what it is: his own self-expression in human words.

That is why the Bible is so tremendously important. Christianity is not a set of clever ideas thought up by wise men of past days, but a faith grounded upon the Word of God, capable of being tested not by human opinion but by *what God has said.* The Bible, 'inspired by God,'[1] is the touchstone of truth. God has spoken —'men moved by the Holy Spirit spoke from God'.[2] In the face of this claim, most of the petty objections to the Bible disappear, and the major and basic one rears its head: that men do not want to know what God has said, because their consciences tell them that it will be too disturbing, too uncomfortable.

But Christians, the men and women of the 'New Way', will treasure it. Believing that through it God speaks to them, they will wish to read it in order to hear his voice. If God has expressed himself fully and adequately through the Bible, then those who are anxious to know him, understand his ways with men and please him in their daily lives, will live by this book. It has been truly said that Christians are the 'people of the Book'.

Dangers and problems

Of course, there will be dangers and problems to be overcome in reading the Bible, and in our general approach to it.

One of the greatest is the most fundamental difficulty of all—*understanding* it. Parts of the Bible are easy enough—narrative, stories, straightforward history—though even here there are deeper, underlying truths that the casual reader may miss. But much of it, especially books like John's Gospel, the letters to the Romans and the Hebrews, Revelation, Ezekiel and Job, is frankly very difficult indeed; not so much because the words or sentences are hard to understand (at least, not in a good, modern translation), but because the ideas being discussed by the writer are so profound and searching. The first eighteen verses of John's Gospel, for instance, do not contain any unusual or difficult words at all in a modern translation, but they make up a passage of incredible depth and wisdom which has stretched and taxed the most brilliant brains of history.

What should we do, then, when we find something in the Bible which we cannot understand—or even a whole passage that makes no sort of sense to us at all? The temptation is to give it up, or just read it mechanically, letting the words by-pass our brains altogether and hoping they will somehow do us some good.

But being discouraged and giving up is the very last thing we should do. If this Book really is God's own explanation of existence, meaning, life and death, then it is bound to be a bit more difficult to understand than a comic strip. Not all of the Bible's ideas can be boiled down to easy slogans and simple illustrations, and only frustration lies ahead for those who expect them to be.

There is a whole series of answers to the problem of understanding the Bible. For most readers, we might put them in the following order.

1. The way you read it. If you picked up a detective story and began it at page 74, it is very likely that much of the book would be meaningless to you. Yet people expect to be able to dip into the Bible here, there and everywhere for Instant Wisdom. Actually the Bible is a consecutive book, or series of books, and the truth in it is *progressive*—that is to say, the picture it gives gets brighter, sharper and clearer as you go through it from the earliest days until the 'last thoughts' of Christ's apostles at the end of the Bible. So we must read consecutively: not necessarily (nor even ideally) from Genesis straight through to Revelation, but noting where the part we are reading fits into the overall scheme of things, and reading through whole books, in sections long enough to provide a context. The Bible yields its riches not to casual prospectors, but to conscientious, methodical miners, who dig deep and take trouble.

2. The way you approach it. Our approach to the Bible often determines success or failure in understanding it. If we come to it in a defeated, agnostic frame of mind ('I suppose I'd better try reading it, but I never understand it and I don't really know that it's all that important anyway'), then we shall get from the Bible exactly what we expected: nothing.

If on the other hand, we come to it in an expectant, believing frame of mind ('This is God's own explanation of truth. It's for me and I'm sure he can help me to understand it.') then our faith will be rewarded.

The determining factor here is faith. Do we believe that this is God's 'Word' to men, or not? If we believe that it is, then it must be capable of being understood by those for whom it is intended. Would God bring into being a book which was beyond the comprehension of those for whom it was written? Do we believe that it was written under the guidance and inspiration of the Holy Spirit? And do we believe that the same Spirit dwells in God's children? If we do, then we have within ourselves and in the Christian community the author himself, to be the perfect interpreter.

If we approach the Bible like this, then the most

natural thing to do will be to talk to God before reading—and during our reading, too, if we come across difficulties. As the hymn puts it, 'God is his own interpreter, and he will make it plain'—provided we ask him, and believe that what we are reading is his own message to us.

Of course, all difficulties will not vanish magically even after prayer. Would we ask God to dig our garden for us while our tools rust in the shed? We cannot expect him to do the other sort of 'spade work' for us either–prayer is no substitute for serious study, but the two should go together. We cannot assume that the Holy Spirit will explain the meaning of a difficult word to us by direct inspiration when a perfectly good dictionary which will give us the same answer stands unopened on our book shelf. In fact, the effort that we put into our study is a good indication of how sincere was our prayer for help. In Paul's vivid phrase, we are to be 'workmen who have no need to be ashamed, rightly handling the word of truth'.[3] The marriage of inspiration and perspiration is always happy and fruitful.

The sort of study aids we shall need will depend to some extent on our education and background, but Bible reading 'Notes' are especially helpful for the beginner, because they divide the text into coherent sections and add both explanation and application.

3. The place you give it. If reading the Bible comes low on our priorities, or is given only a grudging corner in our daily timetable, then we cannot expect to gain more than a superficial grasp of its message. And if we skip group and church Bible studies, or mentally switch off during sermons which attempt to tackle important biblical themes, we are condemning ourselves to an illiterate and ignorant sort of faith. If we believe the Bible is important, then that belief should be backed up by our determination to get to grips with it, not only on our own but together with others who take it seriously.

Superstition

Another, and quite different, kind of danger associated with Bible reading is superstition. Dipping into the Bible for texts, like Jack Horner fishing for plums in his pie, is a dangerous and misleading exercise. The Bible is not a collection of 'texts' or 'verses,' but a complex and complete presentation of the truth. Of course, there are well-known passages which accurately sum up basic Bible truths, but even these must be read in their context—their setting—in order for us to appreciate the full significance of what they are really saying.

The Bible is not magic. It is not a book of spells. It is not a glorified promise box. What God has joined together, man should not put asunder, and that applies to the Scriptures as much as to anything else.

Is the Bible true?

One difficulty, even for Christians, where the Bible is concerned, is doubt about its truth. Most of us live in a society which, when it condescends to mention the Bible at all, pours scorn on it. Science has 'disproved' it. It is just a collection of legends. It is full of mistakes, contradictions and errors. It is brutal and crude. And how do we really know that the book we now have is the Bible God gave?

Most of these questions will come our way sooner or later. Many of them will immediately occur to any intelligent person reading the Bible. It is most important to face them, rather than pushing them out of our minds as 'snares of the devil'.

Has science disproved it?

Probably the short answer to this is that some of the world's most eminent scientists believe whole-heartedly in the Bible's truth and reliability. But that will not do, because even the most brilliant men have been known to practice self-deception.

In fact, science cannot 'disprove' the Bible. 'Science' just means 'knowledge'—organized knowledge, if you like—and the Bible deals with matters of faith impossible to prove or disprove in the scientific sense. Some branches of science may conflict with some parts of the Bible—its history, for example, or its anthropology (the study of man as 'animal')—but that is a million miles from disproving 'the Bible'. So far as this writer is aware, no scientific discovery has yet been made that 'disproves' a single categorical statement of fact in the Bible, so long as both the discovery and the biblical statement are correctly understood. Unhappily, few scientists know the Bible thoroughly, and few biblical scholars know much about science, so that often in the past they have argued at cross-purposes, each misunderstanding what the other was really saying.

It is important in reading the different books of the Bible that we always realize what kind of writing we are dealing with. Some of the Bible is clearly poetry (the Psalms, Job, Proverbs and parts of the prophets, for instance); some is allegory (our Lord's story of the wicked men in the vineyard, for instance), some is visionary (Revelation, for example) and much is a straightforward narrative of history. When Christians say that the Bible is 'true', or is 'the truth', they must mean that it is true *in the sense in which the writer intended it to be understood.* Otherwise what can we make of the Psalmist who calls the heavens a 'tent for the sun'?

However, when the Bible clearly sets out to relate factual truth, we must believe that it is reliable—for what use is a faulty revelation of God? If God gives man a revelation of his truth, then we must suppose that he would take steps to keep that revelation from corruption. Undoubtedly, over the centuries, errors of copying or translation have crept into the versions of the Bible that we have today; but they are not, and cannot be, errors of substance. God has spoken, and what he has said is reliable and authoritative. We would be foolish to claim more for the Bible than God has claimed—an error some Christians have made from time to time. It is not a textbook of physics, botany or zoology. Nor is it a minute guide to the details of the future—a sort of divine old Moore's Almanac.

On the other hand, we would be even more foolish to claim less for the Bible than God has claimed—a far more common error. St. Paul says that 'All scripture is inspired by God and profitable for teaching, for reproof, for correction, and for training in righteousness'.[4] As an inspired guide to truth, as an inspired analysis of my character, and as an inspired manual of moral training, this Book is not simply the Best Buy: it is unique. It is hard to see what effect scientific discoveries could have on that verdict.

A collection of legends?

Most people who accuse the Bible of being a book of 'legends' do not know much about legends. Simply to call something a 'legend' does not necessarily mean that it is untrue, or that it never happened.

But in the common use of the word 'legend', the Bible just does not qualify. It is not a collection of far-fetched stories, or magical mysteries or incredible feats. The Bible's narrative is almost entirely matter-of-fact, with the sensational played down and no attempt at all to convey an atmosphere of romance or excitement. It is about as far as one could imagine from the great legendary sagas of the Greeks or the Norsemen, as anyone who has read such stories and also the Bible will confirm. There one moves in a world of the incredible and bizarre. In the Bible one moves in the real world, with real, fallible human beings in real-life situations.

Of course there are stories in the Bible that have something of this heroic flavour about them—the deeds of Samson, for example. But to dismiss the whole Bible for this reason is to be quite fanatically prejudiced.

Mistakes, contradictions and errors?

It is often argued that the Bible is full of mistakes, contradictions and errors.

No one who really knows the Bible would deny that there are a few places where there are genuine difficulties over apparent contradictions. We have said already that over the centuries errors in copying, or of translation, have certainly crept into the Bible as we now have it. In a few places numbers do not seem to tally and things like genealogies and place names sometimes present problems.

But to say that is not at all to agree that the Bible is 'full' of errors. In fact,it is a staggeringly accurate and consistent book. To the best of my knowledge, wherever modern discovery has thrown light on events, places or people of Bible times, it has confirmed the biblical record. Again to the best of my knowledge, it has never contradicted it. That is a record no history book ever written can equal.

Not only that. Over the years we have become familiar with the fairly short list of 'mistakes, contradictions and errors' of which the Bible is supposed to be 'full.' Not one of them is an error, or apparent error, of any material significance. Not one of them throws any great truth of the Christian faith into doubt.

So, while it is true that there are a number of problems in the Bible arising from apparent mistakes, contradictions and errors, the book as a whole is amazingly consistent, exists substantially as originally written, and is well able to survive close critical scrutiny. After all, for over a hundred years the Bible has been under devastating attack by clever men eager to discredit it. And yet today its reputation and its standing in the eyes of scholars is higher than ever.

Brutal and crude?

Some people make much of the brutality and massacres in the Old Testament, some of which take place apparently at God's command.

Again, we must admit the difficulty. It does seem strange that a God who loves 'the world' and sent his Son to die for sinners should at other times have ordered the massacre of whole tribes.

On the other hand, this objection depends upon two assumptions which are common to almost all human beings, but are not nearly so valid when applied to God. The first is that death is the worst thing that can happen to anybody. The second is that we should be broad-minded about evil.

Worse than death is to be an enemy of God and an ally of evil . . . which is just what many of the idol-worshipping, debased and corrupted tribes of Canaan were like. It may even be that death saved them from far worse judgement by God.

To be tolerant of evil may look like a virtue, but is in fact a vice. If God let evil pass unjudged, allowed the wicked to win not only on earth but in after-life, or looked away when there was injustice or exploitation, he wouldn't be good at all . . . just weak. If, as historians tells us, the tribal people of Canaan, who were pretty well wiped out by the invading people of Israel, were morally corrupt, dissolute, and riddled with venereal disease, to 'tolerate' them would have meant the resulting corruption of Israel too.

The other thing to be said about the Bible's 'crudity' and 'brutality' is that this is only one side of the picture. The parts of the Bible which show us God's severity, judgement and blazing holiness must be balanced by the other parts which show us his gentleness, patience and mercy. The whole Bible gives us a rounded and true 'image' of God; anything less is almost sure to be distorted one way or the other.

Getting down to it

When all is said and done, the best way to answer doubts and difficulties about the Bible is to get down to reading it. If it makes, as it does, tremendous claims for itself ('All scripture is inspired by God . . .'), the best way to judge it is to put its claims to the test.

But don't sit and nibble at it. The Bible has nothing,

or very little, for those who come to it half-heartedly or grudgingly. It is an important book, one of the great books of the world: so give it *time.* If you have fairly recently become a committed Christian that is all the more reason for sticking at it, in order to hear what God is saying to you and to find out his will for your life.

Most of us are grasshoppers mentally. We start one thing, get bored, put it down and then start something else. We find it hard to concentrate, unless we are totally absorbed in what we are doing. Not all of the Bible (to tell the truth, not much of it) is 'entertaining', and it won't rivet the concentration of the average reader unless he feels it is so important that he deliberately sets out to give it his whole attention. Timetables aren't very entertaining, but if you want to catch the right train it's just as well to give them your concentration.

To make it easier to concentrate on the Bible, most of us need a regular time for reading it, a comfortable and undisturbed place, and a mind fresh and alert. Ten minutes at the end of the Late Show, with Dad fuming because he can't find his tooth-paste and your own mind dull with fatigue, is neither the best time nor setting for tackling Paul's Epistle to the Romans. Frankly, you'd find Peanuts a bit demanding in those circumstances.

But a regular daily time, when you are most wide awake and alert, in as quiet a place as you can find, and either sitting comfortably or, if you prefer, kneeling: that is a setting in which you can take the Bible seriously—giving it the sort of attention it deserves.

Of course there are problems in this. For many people it is not possible to read the Bible early in the morning (or late at night!). For some—on shift work, perhaps, or with small children—it is impossible to think in terms of a 'regular' *anything*. For others—in the Armed Services, or in a college dormitory, for example—it may be very difficult to find a quiet or private place in which to read their Bibles and pray.

Of course, this makes things harder, but if we are really taking Bible reading seriously we shall probably find some way round all of these problems. There is no 'magic' hour for reading the Bible. Seven in the morning is no more sacred than noon or ten at night. If the lunch-hour is the most convenient time, pray then. There are no special rewards from God for making it uncomfortable, embarrassing or inconvenient. On the other hand, if we do take the Bible seriously, then nothing will keep us from it for long. Jesus got up long before dawn[5] to pray and talk to God. That's how important he rated it.

At the same time, it is possible to get superstitious about our 'quiet times' (as some people call their private time spent with God in Bible reading and prayer). I remember one girl who worked in my office who would come in sometimes all hot and breathless, having got up late and been forced to rush to work. 'I know today will be awful,' she would say, flopping down at her desk, 'I missed my 'quiet time' this morning.' And sure enough, of course, it *would* be awful, and everything that went wrong would be blamed on that missed 'quiet time', rather than on her inefficiency, or other people's mistakes: very convenient! But God is not a supernatural supervisor, watching our religious productivity and reporting us for any lapses. He is a Father, who perfectly knows and understands our circumstances. He can answer prayers (that is, the real longings of our hearts) that we have not had time to put into words. But naturally he does not answer prayers we can't be bothered to pray!

Part of taking the Bible seriously is to be methodical in reading it. We have mentioned Bible reading Notes (such as those produced by the Scripture Union), and these certainly help us to be methodical, as well as explaining difficulties and applying the 'message.' But whether we use such Notes or not, we ought to have some method or system in our reading. We should decide roughly how much we are going to read each day, and determine to read consecutively through whole books of the Bible, rather than jumping here and there looking for exciting passages. One of the Gospels should come first for 'new' Christians, then perhaps the Acts of the Apostles. For most of the Epistles and for some of the Old Testament the average reader (and even above average people who are unfamiliar with the Bible) will need help to understand it.

A good, modern translation of the Bible is essential equipment. There are enough difficulties in understanding it without adding all the problems of Elizabethan English! The Revised Standard Version is a good modern revision of the 'Authorized' Version, but some others are even nearer everyday speech—especially the Good News Bible, J. B. Phillips' paraphrases, and Kenneth Taylor's *Living Bible.* There is no reason why you should not use several different versions, especially to help you understand difficult passages.

The Bible is a living book, not dead history. If you believe that, you will come to it each time expecting it to speak to your living situation—and it will. Ask God to speak to you through your Bible reading; to show you answers to problems, guidance for action, advice for doubt: and look and listen for his voice. Time and again, in a way that is almost uncanny, you will find this old book speaking to new situations.

To mark the centenary of the Scripture Union I was asked to write a paperback about the way the Bible still speaks to modern people. I invited, through the press, those who had had remarkable or particularly clear-cut experiences of the Bible meeting their needs to write and tell me about them. I received literally hundreds of letters (many of which are quoted in the book[6]), all telling of instances when the Bible had met some specific need in their lives. It would take a very hardened cynic to deny, in the face of these letters, that the Bible is no ordinary book, for it is an impressive body of evidence.

What the Bible did for these people it can do for you —not as you dip here and there for 'mottoes', but as you read it carefully, seriously, systematically and believingly. For those who do that, this remarkable book, the Word of God, is a chief weapon in the 'fight of faith'.

[1] 2 Tim. *3.16*
[2] *2 Peter 1.21*
[3] *2 Tim. 2.15*
[4] *2 Tim. 3.16*
[5] *Mark 1.35*
[6] *For All the People* (Hodder and Stoughton)

SELF-CHECK TEST 3

Circle the letter of the correct answer for each of the following. Choose the answer which most completely expresses the truth taught in the chapter.

1. God speaks to us chiefly through
a. the medium of prayer.
b. the Bible.
c. the circumstances of life.
d. worship.

2. Since God is good, personal and infinite, it logically follows that
a. he is too remote and 'too busy' to communicate with such 'tiny specks of matter' such as we are.
b. he could conceivably communicate with us but the chances of his actually doing so are slim.
c. he can, must and does communicate with us.
d. he communicates with us but we cannot respond.

3. The Bible's chief function is to
a. reveal to us vital truths which we need to know about ourselves, God and our relationship to him.
b. reveal to us future events.
c. cast light upon the religious history of the human race.
d. arbitrate in the moral struggle in our conscience.

4. The major and basic reason why people reject the Bible is that they
a. cannot understand it.
b. dislike what it has to say.
c. believe it to be a collection of myths and fables.
d. prefer other literature.

5. The Bible is often difficult to understand because
a. of the words that are used.
b. of the sentence structure which it employs.
c. the language in which it was written is foreign to us.
d. of the profound and revolutionary ideas it conveys.

6. When we approach the Bible we should
a. ask God to be 'his own interpreter'.
b. expect to face no difficulties if we pray for God's insight.
c. set aside every man-made tool for Bible study and rely solely on the Holy Spirit.
d. depend solely on 'notes' to explain what we read.

7. When reading the Bible it is important to
a. accept every single statement as literal and absolute.
b. dismiss as untrue any statement which appears unscientific.
c. realize that the category of writing (poetry, allegory, vision, history, etc.) will determine whether or not the portion is true.
d. understand that what is said is truth in the sense in which the writer intended it to be understood.

8. In the controversy between science and the Bible our attitude should be
a. Evidently the Bible contains copyist's errors, therefore not even its major teachings can be implicitly trusted.
b. The Bible is only reliable as a guide to truth and morals.
c. The Bible is reliable, since God can be trusted to ensure that his revelation is not misleading.
d. The Bible can be looked upon as scientific and is therefore an exhaustive guide to physics, botany, astronomy, etc.

9. The alleged brutalities in the Bible are to be explained
a. as apocryphal since these incidents are not consistent with God's character as revealed in the Bible.
b. as proof that God cannot be wholly good.
c. in the light of the cultural evolution of the Hebrew religion.
d. on the ground that God's perspective is higher, holier and more complete than ours.

10. The best time to read the Bible is
a. first thing in the morning.
b. the last thing at night.
c. at a convenient but regular time.
d. morning, noon and night.

4
WHAT IS PRAYER?

A conversation has to be two-way—otherwise it is simply a monologue. If the Bible is the main way God speaks to us, then prayer is the main way we speak to God. Yet this is one aspect of the Christian life that people very often find extraordinarily difficult. Those who can casually chatter away to their friends and relatives dry up when they are alone with God.

But why? In one sense prayer is a 'natural' activity. Often little children pray fluently and easily—though at a very simple level, of course. But for the adult Christian it becomes a mechanical operation, done because one is 'supposed to', or an arid exercise in mental discipline, rather than a living expression of a warm and personal relationship between a Father and his son or daughter. New Christians often ask, 'But what do I pray about?' Older Christians ask, 'What is the point of it all?' There are countless books on the subject, and advice about prayer is endless, yet still many, many Christians have to admit that their prayer life is unsatisfying and unreal.

Diagnosis: What has gone wrong?

The first step in curing any malady is to diagnose it accurately—to establish exactly what is wrong. Most of us who have prayer problems simply blame ourselves for lack of zeal or holiness, and screw up our wills to 'do better'. It is safe to say that that is a sure way to do worse! Prayer is not a matter of effort, nor—essentially, and whatever the devotional manuals say—of discipline. A forced, artificial conversation is of no value in terms of building a living friendship. If we have to compel ourselves to talk to someone ('I really must try to pray for at least fifteen minutes every day') then there is something seriously wrong with our 'love' for them. Can you imagine a husband resolving to talk to his wife for 'at least fifteen minutes' before going to bed each night?

Prayer flows naturally from a right relationship with God, and, in the process, helps to deepen and strengthen the relationship. If we find prayer hard or dry, it is the relationship that is wrong (or our understanding of it), not our prayer system or discipline. Unconfessed and unrepented sin[1], wrong attitudes towards our fellow Christians[2], an inadequate sense of gratitude at God's love in saving us[3]: these are the sort of flaws in our relationship to God which kill prayer.

But if our relationship with him is right, and we are walking with him trustingly, confessing sin as it arises, and constantly thankful for his goodness and generosity to us, then we should be able to enjoy prayer. Supposing, however, that we still do not. What then? There are a number of answers to give.

The most probable has been hinted at already. With many people it is not that their relationship with God is 'wrong', in itself, but that their understanding of it is faulty. They are truly trusting in Jesus Christ, faithfully repenting sins, and are profoundly thankful for their salvation—but God seems distant and their understanding of him is clouded by serious misconceptions. In some cases they are unable to think of him at all in personal terms—and it is very hard to pray to a 'Being'. In other cases they are obsessed with his transcendence (that is, the fact that he is infinitely 'above' us), and cannot dare to draw near to him. In yet other cases they are overwhelmed with a sense of their own sinfulness and unworthiness and shrink from his presence.

Now all of these are misunderstandings, not of ourselves but of God and his dealings with human beings. Let's take them one at a time.

God as a Person

It is far too easy to describe prayer as 'talking to God' as though that solved all the problems. The difficulty for most of us is that we are used to talking to people we can see, face to face, or at least visualize—say on the other end of a phone. But 'no one has seen God at any time'.[4] He is immortal, invisible. 'God is spirit.'[5] How can we 'talk' to a 'Being' who is infinite?

We have already argued that the Christian God is personal—not just a vague force or power, but a person, with all the marks of personality. But it is one thing to believe that as an article of the faith, and quite another to be able to talk with such a person naturally and intimately. Yet if we cannot talk with him, our prayer will become stilted and unreal—not at all the expression of a warm and deep relationship.

For most Christians the only answer is to think of

God in terms of his Son Jesus Christ. After all, Jesus himself said, 'He who has seen me has seen the Father'[6]. St. Paul says that 'in him the whole fulness of deity dwells bodily.'[7] If human eyes cannot see the Father, human eyes have seen the Son, who 'bears the very stamp of his nature'.[8] We cannot visualize God, who 'dwells in unapproachable light, whom no man has ever seen or can see'.[9] But we can visualize his Son Jesus, walking the lanes of Galilee, talking with his friends, healing the sick, weeping beside a tomb or touching a leper to make him whole. If we think of Jesus Christ when we pray—and especially if we read about his words or his actions just before we turn to prayer—we shall find it easier to talk to his Father *through him.*

God above us

At the same time, thinking of the Lord Jesus Christ will help to counter the feeling that God is tremendously distant from us. He is, of course, infinitely 'above' us, in the moral sense, and obviously there is a vast gulf between people like ourselves and a God of purity and holiness. But it was precisely to span that gulf that Jesus Christ came. He, as the divine Man—truly human, fully divine—restored the broken link between fallen mankind and its God. Through Jesus Christ, God is very near us—indeed, within us. There is no unbridgeable gulf any longer!

Similarly, because Jesus Christ died for our sins, they are no longer a barrier between us and God. To act as though they were is to imply that what Jesus Christ did on the Cross was not good enough. Of course we are 'unworthy' to come to him—utterly unworthy. But he invites us to come, forgiven and cleansed through his Son, not hesitantly or nervously, but confidently and happily. 'We have confidence to enter the sanctuary (God's presence) by the blood of Jesus . . . let us draw near with a true heart in full assurance of faith.'[10]

What shall I pray about?

Once our attitude and approach to God in prayer is right, we may wonder, 'What should I pray about?' From childhood, many people have got the idea that prayer is a sort of spiritual shopping list, when we detail our needs and wants and ask God to do something about them. We may add a few 'thanks' for favours received, but most of our prayer is taken up with requests.

Now there is nothing wrong with making requests to God in prayer. He has invited us to do so.[11] But it is a travesty of prayer to think of it simply in these terms. Indeed, if you have followed through what we have said about attitudes and approach, you will probably agree that to pray like this is not just to misunderstand prayer, but to misunderstand God.

In a sense, 'What should I pray about?' is an unanswerable question. Normal husbands do not ask themselves, 'What can I talk about to my wife?' The conversation flows naturally out of their relationship. Though not at that level, our praying should be nearer to conversation than to catalogue.

For the beginner, the best approach is probably simply to tell God about the day, about yourself, about problems or pleasures, about things that may crop up—in short, to bring him into the whole circle of your daily life. In doing this, you will almost certainly begin to find yourself bringing in other aspects of prayer—sins will be confessed, the sorrows and needs of your friends will be shared and brought to God, thankfulness will be expressed. So, quite naturally, a properly balanced prayer life will start to develop, built upon the foundation of a real and living relationship.

Part of that balance will be what is called 'intercession'—praying for others. The word literally means putting yourself between God and them, on their behalf. This is a creative and wonderful experience, which ought to involve us in real commitment to those for whom we pray. If I am praying sincerely for somebody, and caring about them, then my whole attitude towards them will be transformed. In other words, my prayer not only changes their situation (as God hears and answers it, and helps them) but it also changes me. People thousands of miles apart, who have only met once or twice (and in some cases never), have experienced a deep and genuine unity and fellowship in Christ simply through praying for each other.

If we are praying for people in this way, we shall probably not need the complicated 'prayer lists' and 'prayer cycles' which some Christians favour. There seems to be something artificial and mechanical about them. I don't need written reminders to think about people I love. However, many people who are experts in the 'art' of prayer find some list or system valuable, so it is probably unwise to dismiss the idea completely.

What is important is that we should not become slaves to any system of prayer. Any scheme or list ought to be flexible, and from time to time we should 'liberate' our time of prayer completely, by opening our minds to God and simply sharing with him all we are, all we long to be for him, and all we desire for others.

Discovering God's will

One of the problems of prayer is the whole idea of praying 'according to God's will.'[12] Obviously there's no future in praying against it, so discovering what God wants (as distinct from what we want) becomes tremendously important. Even our Lord once prayed in these terms—'Father, *if thou art willing,* remove this cup from me; nevertheless, not my will, but thine, be done.'[13]

There is no point in getting worried about this. If we have accepted Jesus Christ as our Lord, and are consciously obeying him, then God—who is almighty—won't let us get out of his will. The only harm we shall do by praying for something he doesn't want for us is that we shall waste some time!

On the other hand, Christians usually learn to recognize when God is 'laying something on their hearts'—one of those odd religious phrases that cannot be translated into 'normal' English. We become aware that our prayers are being taken over by him. We feel as though we are co-operating with him. When words seem to fail us, he interprets our thoughts for us. At times like this we realize what 'praying according to his will' really means—but this does not mean we give up praying at other times just because we have not yet grasped God's will for any particular matter.

Often God's will is obvious. We know, for instance, that he wishes us to be 'holy.'[14] We know that he wishes 'all men to be saved.'[15] We know that he wishes to give his Holy Spirit to those who ask him.[16] So requests such as these may always be considered as in line with his will. And we don't have to wait for a supernatural sign from heaven before we start asking God to help us overcome sin.

It is not harmful, however, and it is probably valuable, to use prayer as a means of discovering God's will where we are not clear about it. 'Is this your will, Father?' is a prayer of humility and dependence, and one we should all utter from time to time. Equally, it is healthy to add the phrase 'If it is your will' to requests which are not obviously God's will, or about which we have not been given any certainty.

What words do I use?

It is amazing how many people are still afraid to pray—even privately, let alone in company—because they feel they can't express themselves properly. This is like the people who used to stay away from church because they had no Sunday clothes. God gave us the gift of language, and can understand whatever we say, or intend to say. After all, he reads our thoughts, so he is not going to have problems interpreting our words!

There is no 'special' language for addressing God, and there never has been. Moses talked with God 'as though he was his friend.'[17] The language of prayer in the New Testament is the language of the street corner and the marketplace. It is very sad that so many people since then have preferred and used a special and almost artificial language for prayer—even their private prayers— and have felt that they cannot address God properly unless they can master the complicated use of 'thee's,' 'thou's' and 'thine's,' with all the odd verbal forms that go with them ('Wouldest,' 'camest' and so on).

Human eloquence may move us, but it cuts no ice with God. Our prayers are no more likely to be answered for being expressed in fancy words. In fact, if words fail us, or we can't think how to express some deep longing, God hears, interprets and answers our 'sighs and groans'.

Sometimes, when I hear Christians at public prayer gatherings raising their voices, pounding their hands, or pleading in colourful and passionate language with God, I feel that my own prayers must sound very dull and matter-of-fact. But then I remind myself that such eloquence and passion can only help the other people present (or the speaker), but can have no influence with God at all beyond the actual desire, longing or need that lies behind them.

Of course forceful language and memorable phrases are a great help in congregational prayer, because they focus the ideas better than woolly or vague language. But their value is for us, not God. Obviously we should always try to offer him our best, and I am not suggesting that we deliberately or casually use ugly, crude or inaccurate language in prayer. But it would be a terrible misunderstanding of what prayer is all about, and what God is like, to hold back from praying because we 'can't find the right words'.

When you turn to prayer, say what is in your heart, just as you would to a trusted and respected friend. Like a friend, God is anxious to listen, not reluctant, and certainly not critical of the words you use to express true and sincere feelings and longings.

Wandering thoughts

Quite often Christians get very worried because they find their thoughts wandering when they are 'supposed' to be praying. Rightly, they feel that this shows a lack of respect or love for God. After all, our thoughts don't usually wander when we are talking to someone we love or admire. Wrongly, however, they don't get beyond feeling guilty about their lack of concentration.

It is worth asking why we concentrate on anything. Usually it is because it is obviously important to us (however boring), or extremely interesting (however unimportant). We give our undivided attention to the boss (because he is important) or to our closest friend (because he interests us). On both counts, God ought to have our fullest concentration. He is obviously important, and 'interesting'.

So what goes wrong?

There are some simple and practical explanations, of course. Sometimes we try to pray when we are too sleepy, and then we fall asleep in mid-sentence. Sometimes we get carried away by a train of thought started off by an item of prayer, and our grasshopper minds go leaping away after it. Sometimes we pray when our minds are full of other things, or in circumstances where we are easily distracted. In each of these cases the remedy is fairly obvious.

To avoid falling asleep while praying, we choose our prayer time for an hour of the day when we are not tired. If our minds get distracted by some of our prayer topics, we must discipline our thinking, or else turn the very distraction into prayer. (For example, supposing I am praying about money, including the mortgage on the house—and find myself distracted into a line of thought which ends up with redecorating the living room. Probably the best answer is to turn this into a prayer—about whether it would be right to spend money on wallpaper at this moment.)

The time and location of prayer are important. If we pray when our minds are racing away on many important topics—say, immediately after an important business meeting—then it will obviously be harder for us to concentrate. Noisy surroundings, or people coming in and out, can also make concentration difficult. Some people can do nothing about this—these are their circumstances, and God understands and makes allowances. But if we could avoid them, but choose not to bother, then we may run into trouble.

The right time of day—when we are alert, but not too involved in the day's affairs; the right place—private and quiet; the right attitude—giving God the attention he deserves: these are the major answers to wandering thoughts.

Perhaps one might add that some apparently minor details can affect our concentration. For instance, the tradition (it is no more) that we should pray with our eyes shut is not a help to everybody. Sometimes to look at a picture (of a person for whom we are praying) a cross or even a map can be a great aid to concentration. Equally, our physical posture for prayer can be more important than we imagine. If we are too comfortable, we may relax and fall asleep, or doze. If we are very uncomfortable (bare knees on a hard floor) we shall be distracted by the very discomfort. Sitting or kneeling, we should aim at a position which combines reverence for the Person we are talking with and reasonable comfort.

Unanswered prayer

Sooner or later—probably sooner—we shall come across the very real problem of 'unanswered prayer'. What we really mean by this is prayer that is answered in the negative. We ask perhaps for the recovery of a sick relative—and instead he dies. Many people who have talked to me about their loss of 'faith' trace it back to an incident like this.

If you have followed what we have been saying about God, and also what we have been saying about prayer, you will probably see at once that yet again the answer is more basic than the simple allegation that 'God refused to answer my prayer'. It lies in the relationship between ourselves and God, and in our understanding of the nature of God himself.

James, in his epistle, says, 'You ask and do not receive, because you ask wrongly, to spend it on your passions.' In other words, one straightforward explanation of 'unanswered' prayer is that it is selfish prayer. Selfish prayer is prayer that does not have as its main aim bringing about God's will, whether in my own life, or somebody else's, or in some situation or event.

If, as we have argued, God knows all, and is all-powerful, then prayer is really a matter of getting in gear with his wishes and co-operating with the one who knows best. Once we have seen that, our prayer can never be selfish, because we have admitted that his will is best for us and for others, and whether we are praying for them, or for ourselves, it is that perfect will of a perfect and all-knowing God that we are really asking for.

The trouble is that we often think we know what God's will ought to be! To go back to the example of a relative who is ill, we automatically assume that God's will is his recovery. That is because, for us, death seems to be the worst thing that can happen to anyone. But it isn't to God, and he knows best. That may sound rather hard (and, from a human being, I suppose it is). But one day we shall realize that our sixty or seventy years on earth are only a tiny fraction of our living, and God sees the whole of our existence in both time and eternity.

Father and Son

Prayer is, basically, dependence on God. It is a moment-by-moment, day-by-day admission that we cannot 'do it ourselves'. It is the expressed need of a child to his parent.

A father was taking his five year old son for a walk in the country. They came to a stream, and Junior decided that he couldn't jump across it.

'Daddy, I can't jump across. You'll have to lift me.'

There is the dependence of the child—'I can't, but you can.' This is the heart of a realistic attitude to God in prayer.

Later on the same walk Junior spotted an ice-cream vendor, and demanded a lolly: 'Daddy, can I have a lolly?'

There is the prayer of investigation. 'Is it your will for me to have this?' Junior knows very well that if it is not his father's will he will have to go without, because he has no money of his own to buy it with. Many of our prayers will in fact be prayers of investigation, as we seek to find God's will in different situations. Again, the very question asked makes a huge implication—that the person asked knows what is best, and is the only one who can meet our request.

The walk over, father and Junior got home, where a good, nourishing meal was waiting for them. Junior pitched in hungrily, and was soon asking: 'Daddy, can I have a second helping?'

This is the prayer of faith. Junior knows his father's will—that he should grow up big and strong, and that dad likes him to eat a second helping. So his request is co-operation with his father's known will—the 'perfect' prayer, which is always answered positively.

There come such times for every Christian—when his prayer becomes co-operation with the known will of his Father, and the answer to his prayer is a foregone conclusion.

Here, then, are three elements of prayer: investigation, dependence and co-operation. We cast ourselves upon God, who can do for us what we can never do for ourselves. We want to know his will, because he knows best and he alone can meet our needs. And when we know his will—either because he has already told us it in the Bible, or has made it plain to us—then we co-operate by lining ourselves up with it in prayer, praise and action.

[1] *Psalm 66.18*
[2] *Philippians 2.2, 3*
[3] *Philippians 4.6*
[4] *John 1.18*
[5] *John 4.24*
[6] *John 14.9*
[7] *Col. 2.9*
[8] *Heb. 1.3*
[9] *I Tim. 6.16*
[10] *Heb. 10.19-22*
[11] *Matt. 7.7*
[12] *I John 5.14*
[13] *Luke 22.42*
[14] *I Pet. 1.15*
[15] *I Tim. 2.4*
[16] *Luke 11.13*
[17] *Exodus 33.11*

SELF-CHECK TEST 4

Circle the letter of the correct answer for each of the following. Choose the answer which most completely expresses the truth taught in the chapter.

1. Basically, a natural prayer life flows from
a. greater zeal and holiness.
b. a more disciplined life.
c. a right relationship with God.
d. a desire to get something we need.

2. A misunderstanding of our relationship with God is to
a. think that God is too distant to be interested in us.
b. be so aware of our sinfulness that we shrink from him.
c. hold abstract, vague and impersonal concepts of God.
d. All or any of the above.

3. The ideal way to think of God as a person when we pray is to
a. keep on repeating the positive principle 'God is a person'.
b. imagine him as a larger, holier and more accomplished extension of our own persons.
c. visualize him as having become a true human being in the person of Jesus Christ.
d. have an image or a picture of him to look at when we pray.

4. The proper attitude towards prayer should be that
a. it is an opportunity to list before God items of current need.
b. it is a duty to be performed and should be done as regularly and as thoroughly as possible.
c. it is to be conducted with the utmost formality, since God is holy, sovereign and awesome.
d. based on a real, living relationship, it should be natural.

5. Intercession is the art of
a. presenting before God my own personal needs.
b. praying for others.
c. persuading God to take an interest in my friends.
d. getting others to pray for me.

6. Praying 'according to God's will'
a. only takes place when we feel subjectively that our prayers are being 'taken over' by him.
b. is of some importance but is not absolutely vital since God's will is always accomplished in the end.
c. should be a source of constant concern to us since there is no point at all in praying against God's will.
d. may be subjective, but is often an objective matter since much of God's will has already been revealed to us.

7. When considering what language to use to God we should remember that
a. fine language and memorable phrases are never of any value.
b. we should always address him as 'Thou' rather than 'You'.
c. God can read our thoughts, so he can certainly understand what we say no matter in what language it is expressed.
d. God can interpret even our signs and groans; therefore verbalizing of prayers is unnecessary.

8. Wandering thoughts in prayer can best be arrested
a. by remembering that God is both important and interesting.
b. by choosing either a comfortable seat or a hard floor so long as our posture runs counter to our natural inclination.
c. by resolving not to be distracted at any cost.
d. by using a prayer list.

9. If the thing for which we are praying does not happen the way we wish, or the exact opposite happens, then
a. it is a clear case of unanswered prayer.
b. it proves that prayer is pointless.
c. it means that the prayer was answered in the negative by a God who knows best.
d. it is one of those insoluble mysteries which are inherent in the Christian faith.

10. Three elements in prayer described in this chapter are
a. asking, waiting, receiving.
b. talking, listening, accepting.
c. investigating, depending, co-operating.
d. kneeling, feeling, healing.

5
WHAT CAN I *DO* FOR GOD?

The Bible, prayer, Christian fellowship—in the church, at the Lord's Table and informally, too—these are basic ingredients in living the Christian life. In this chapter we are thinking about a further vital ingredient in this life; not, this time, something given by God, but something we do in obedience to him which brings tremendous blessings into our lives as we do it. This 'something' is Christian service.

Time and again in the New Testament Christians are called 'servants'—or, more correctly, 'slaves'. We 'serve the Lord Christ'.[1] The service we offer has many different aspects, but fundamental to them all is the notion that he is our Lord as well as our Saviour. For our purpose we are going to divide this 'service' into three parts: confession, witness and work.

Confession

'If you confess with your lips Jesus as Lord, and believe in your heart that God raised him from the dead you will be saved,' says Paul.[2] This makes 'confessing' Christ very important. In fact, it implies that if no one knows you are a Christian—you have never 'confessed him with your lips'—then you may not be 'saved' at all.

What does 'confessing' mean? Quite simply, it means openly admitting your private, personal faith in Jesus Christ. For most Christians in the early Church this was done when they were baptized, as they stood before their fellow-Christians and said something very simple and definite, such as 'Jesus is Lord'. Today it is equally possible to confess Christ in baptism or confirmation, or a similar occasion at which Christians are given an opportunity to stand up and admit to their faith.

However, confessing is not simply a once-for-all matter, to be forgotten after we have let a few of our fellow-Christians know where we stand. After all, the opposite of 'confess' is 'deny'. While the possibility of denying Christ is present—and that means until our dying day—the need for confessing is also present. Every time our faith is questioned we make a choice between denying or confessing Christ.

One girl who worked in a typing pool told me that for years after she became a Christian she was faced with this choice every Monday morning. When the girls got to work they would talk about what they had been doing over the weekend. When they asked her what she had been doing, she would always avoid admitting that she had been to church, because she was embarrassed to think what their reaction would be. So—without actually mentioning his name—she failed to confess Christ every Monday morning; indeed, she denied him.

So, to confess him is a continuing attitude of openness about our faith. It is a willingness to be known for what we are, to take our stand for our Lord, to 'nail our colours to the mast.' 'For every one who acknowledges me before men, I also will acknowledge before my Father who is in heaven.'[3]

Witness

Witness is a stage further than confession. You can't be a Christian at all if you fail to confess Christ, but to fail to witness is simply a mark of weak or uncertain faith. As people often misunderstand what is involved in witnessing to Christ, I want to set out the biblical picture of it first.

A 'witness,' in New Testament terms, is someone who has had a personal experience of the risen Christ, and is prepared to testify to it.[4] Actually, by the very meaning of the word, a witness cannot testify to second-hand knowledge. It must be something he has seen, heard or experienced himself, or his testimony is invalid.

By that definition, every real Christian is a potential witness to the resurrection of Jesus Christ. He knows that Christ is alive by personal experience, and can speak of what he has seen and heard.

This witness can be made in various ways. In a sense, we are all witnesses all the time—even when we are silent. For the sort of people we are speaks eloquently of the sort of Master we follow. If our lives are shabby, petty and dull, then that is the picture of Jesus Christ people will get from us. If our hypocrisy is our best known feature, then again we are bearing a bad testimony to Christ. On the other hand, if people speak well of us, or have to admit that we live consistent, sincere lives, that bears a good testimony to Christ.

The silent witness of my life is the most important one I have to offer. There can be no doubt about that. My most moving words, if they are unmatched by actions, or contradicted by them, will count for nothing. But the silent witness depends upon my daily confession of Christ, for if those around me do not know that I belong to him, then my sincere, consistent life brings credit to me, but no honour for him, and therefore is completely valueless as witness.

Witness by word is also vital in a wider sense—beyond simply confessing my faith, that is. Peter puts it like this: 'Always be prepared to make a defence to any one who calls you to account for the hope that is in you, yet do it with gentleness and reverence.'[5]

Here the Christian is being told to do more than simply admit that he is a Christian. He is also being told to do more than simply (though 'simply' is the wrong word) live a consistent, sincere life before his fellow men. He is being told to answer with words those who ask him to explain his faith and his actions; to 'give an account' of himself.

It is worth pointing out that this is to be in response to an inquiry ('to any one who calls you to account'), rather than an aggressive verbal onslaught on an unsuspecting victim. While some Christians are undoubtedly called to the work of evangelism, and are gifted by God in approaching people with the gospel message, that is evangelism rather than witness (yes, there *is* a difference). For the ordinary believer, the call of God is to confess Christ, live a consistent Christian life, and be ready to explain and account for his faith to any one who inquires. If we all did that, and did it all the time, then one suspects the work of the evangelists would be a great deal easier—and the impact of the Church on the community would be enormous.

But to give this 'verbal defence' requires knowledge.

Many Christians who stay silent about their faith do so, not out of fear, but out of ignorance. They dare not speak because they do not know. So a necessary first step towards this sort of witness is a good, sound grasp of the basic biblical doctrines, especially those that relate to personal salvation and assurance. By this much more is implied than merely memorizing a few proof texts. Nothing less than a good working knowledge of the Bible's teaching on God, man, sin and salvation in Christ will be adequate when an intelligent modern person confronts us with a demand for an explanation of our faith.

So we should give time to mastering Christian doctrine, and learning how to defend and justify our position as believers. We must be careful that this does not make us rude, aggressive or opinionated. As Peter puts it, we are to bear our witness with 'gentleness and reverence'—and that means reverence ('respect') for the other, unbelieving person. Our Lord was the perfect witness to his Father, because he succeeded in being clear-cut, definite and uncompromising where truth was concerned, but yet gentle, courteous and dignified in dealing with individuals. He never regarded them as scalps to be collected or objects to be manipulated, but as persons, each requiring a different approach.

Our witness should be like his—clear-cut and definite, but marked by a real humility. After all, we have sat where they sit, we have been outside the kingdom of God, we also have sinned and fallen short of God's glory. We are no better, and no more deserving, than they are. If God has been patient and merciful to us, then he can be to them. We should regard them as objects of his love, and therefore of ours, as well.

Yet this respect for the 'other person', and humility of approach, must not be used as an excuse for silence or timidity. In the very same passage as we have been quoting, Peter prefaces his words about witness with this advice: 'Have no fear of them, nor be troubled, but in your hearts reverence Christ as Lord.'[6] While we are to respect those to whom we witness, we are not to be afraid of them, nor let our fear of their reaction embarrass or silence us. It is possible to react so extremely against the aggressive, insensitive 'Brother, are you saved?' sort of witness that we fail to witness at all. The balance struck by Peter himself is the one to aim at—'Do not be afraid of them ... but in your hearts reverence Christ as Lord.... Make a defence to any one who calls you to account for the hope that is in you, yet do it with gentleness and reverence.'

Service

Christian service is always two-way—to God, and to other people. We 'serve the Lord Christ,'[7] but also, as Paul puts it, we are '*your* servants for Jesus' sake.'[8] In more vivid language, our Lord expressed the same double duty. 'Truly I say to you, as you did it to one of the least of these my brethren, you did it to me.'[9] The 'it' was feeding the hungry, clothing the naked, and visiting the sick or imprisoned, and Jesus was saying that to do these things to those in need was the same as doing them for him.

This service is not a grudging duty, but a natural expression of our love for and dependence on Christ. He spent his life for others, healing them, helping them, talking with them and finally dying for them. He was the 'Man for others.' That is why his followers too must be involved in the needs of others, continuing his work in the world of touching men and making them whole. Our Lord's work of salvation was finished, once and for all, on the cross. His ministry among men and women has not ended, but now he continues it through his own people. We are his hands, his feet and his strong arms, still present in the world.

To serve in his name is not only to be a help to others, but also and incidentally to strengthen our own faith. Young Christians who have spent their vacations at work camps—painting a mission hospital, perhaps, or building a refugee camp, or cleaning out slums in an inner city ghetto—have given something priceless to their fellow-men, but they have also received something priceless from God himself. There is a grace in *going and doing* that can never be received while sitting and meditating. It is probably linked with the obedience involved in carrying out a clear command of the Lord himself.

[1] *Col. 3.24*
[2] *Rom. 10.9*
[3] *Matt. 10.32*
[4] *Acts 4.33*
[5] *I Peter 3.15*
[6] *I Peter 3.14, 15*
[7] *Col. 3.24*
[8] *2 Cor. 4.5*
[9] *Matt. 25.40*

SELF-CHECK TEST 5

Circle the letter of the correct answer for each of the following. Choose the answer which most completely expresses the truth taught in the chapter.

1. In the New Testament, Christians are frequently called
a. heralds.
b. partners.
c. friends.
d. slaves.

2. The need for confessing Jesus as Lord is stated in
a. John 3.16.
b. Romans 10.9.
c. Ephesians 2.20.
d. 1 Timothy 1.15.

3. Confessing Christ
a. is optional for the believer.
b. is done once and for all at the time of baptism or confirmation.
c. is a continuing confession of faith in Christ.
d. is satisfactorily accomplished when we admit we go to church regularly.

4. Witnessing for Christ
a. is identical with confessing Christ.
b. is testifying to a personal experience with Christ.
c. is essential, for without such witness it is impossible to be a Christian at all.
d. is less important than confessing Christ.

5. Witness by word of mouth
a. is not an important aspect of the Christian life.
b. is fully discharged when we confess Christ as Saviour.
c. involves giving an account of our faith and actions.
d. implies aggressively 'pushing' our faith on to other people.

6. Being equipped to witness involves
a. acquiring a thorough grasp of basic Biblical doctrine.
b. mastering a few 'proof texts'.
c. nothing except dependence on the Holy Spirit.
d. attending a Bible School.

7. Our Lord was the perfect witness because
a. he gave a definite, uncompromising witness about his Father.
b. he was gentle, courteous and dignified in dealing with those he contacted.
c. he treated people as individuals and approached each one differently.
d. he did all the above.

8. In witnessing we should adopt
a. the 'Brother, are you saved?' approach.
b. the 'I'll leave it to the extrovert type' approach.
c. the 'I don't care what people think' approach.
d. the 'I'll respect them, but not fear them' approach.

9. Christian service
a. is reserved for full time Christian workers.
b. is simply and solely a matter of showing concern for the social needs of others.
c. involves serving the Lord in the very act of serving men.
d. relates only to sacred things and has nothing to do with social action.

10. Serving the Lord
a. is far less important than sitting and meditating on the Word of God.
b. necessarily involves each believer in surrendering vacations to slum work, hospital visitation, participating in Christian camps, etc.
c. strengthens our own faith.
d. is optional since we are under grace, not law.

6 WHAT IF I HAVE PROBLEMS?

Books of advice, like this one, usually give a great deal of space to 'problems'. The reason is that in anything worth while there are bound to be hang-ups, and it is at those points that we need help. The Christian life is not just a series of problems to be overcome. We must get that clear. But problems will come, and this chapter looks at some of the most common ones that may turn up in the first year or two of Christian experience (and later, too, for that matter). The main answer to all of them is 'Don't panic!'

Failure

Many people put off accepting Christ for fear that they will not be able to 'keep it up'. Others, having taken the step, suddenly find that they are falling short of what they have decided are 'Christian standards'.

Sometimes this is the fault of sincere but over-enthusiastic preachers and evangelists, who give the impression that once you are converted all your problems, sins and failures will end. It is a nasty anti-climax to an encounter with Christ to discover that, far from ending, they present themselves in new and disturbing ways. In a sense, a non-Christian has no 'problem' with sin, because he may not believe that it has serious moral consequences. But once we accept Christ, sin becomes a major problem, for we find that our new 'nature', the part of us that is 'born of the Spirit', is in conflict with our old nature, the part of us that is fallen and earthly. Our old nature is dead, but it won't lie down.

Many new Christians are shattered to find that perhaps within hours of accepting Christ they have sinned, possibly quite seriously. They feel that this proves that they are not Christians at all, that their experience was phony and their new faith invalid. In fact it proves nothing of the kind.

The new Christian is the immediate object of enemy counter-attack. The spiritual powers of evil—and don't ever under-estimate them—will do all they can to dismay you and discredit your commitment to Christ. Probably never before will you have been so conscious of the reality of sin and temptation.

Your conscience will be more active, too, because the Holy Spirit has breathed new life into it. This may well mean that things you did before without any qualms you now recognize as sinful and blameworthy.

All of these factors will combine to taunt you with your failure. 'Call yourself a Christian?' the inward sneer will whisper, 'And you do things like *that*?' If you were not forewarned, the effect might be to throw you completely, and make you cast doubts on what God has done in your life.

In fact, the Bible specifically states that Christians will sin (though it is contrary to their new nature), and it even tells us what remedial steps to take.

'If we say we have no sin, we deceive ourselves, and the truth is not in us. If we confess our sins, he is faithful and just, and will forgive our sins and cleanse us from all unrighteousness. . . . My little children, I am writing this to you so that you may not sin; but if any one does sin, we have an advocate with the Father, Jesus Christ the righteous; and he is the expiation for our sins, and not for ours only but also for the sins of the whole world.'[1]

These words were written to Christians, who were told to be realistic and honest about their failures. That is the real answer to sin in the Christian—openness and honesty to God about it. 'If we confess. . . .' There is the problem. Our natural tendency is to deny (as we saw on the subject of Christian witness). We automatically begin to excuse ourselves as soon as we are accused of anything wrong. But with God, what is required is not explanation, but expiation—and that means the price already paid by Jesus Christ so that our sins (past, present and future) could be forgiven. Only when we are prepared to admit our guilt can the remedy be applied. The one fatal barrier to forgiveness is unwillingness to repent.

'Repentance' is not a word in common use, but it is a key word in the Christian life. Its basic meaning is a complete reversal of attitude, a total about-turn. In connection with a single act of sin or disobedience, it means that we reverse our attitude (of disobedience or self-justification) and admit that God is right when he calls what we have done 'sin'. To repent is to agree with God's verdict on our failure, instead of making excuses. It really is as simple as that.

It is, of course, easier said than done. If we have

spoken spitefully about a colleague, we shall probably then suppress any guilty feelings about it by arguing—to others, or to ourselves—that he 'asked for it', that it was 'righteous anger', or that we did it in the other person's long-term interests. But the Holy Spirit keeps at us, reminding us about what the Bible says on the subject of wild or cruel words, until finally—perhaps hours, even days, later—we end our arrogant resistance and say to God. 'All right. You win. I was wrong. It was a sin to speak about Ted like that. Please forgive me, for Christ's sake.' At that moment, but not before, the 'blood of Jesus Christ his Son cleanses us from all sin.'

Some people argue that this is forgiveness 'on the cheap'—that to make it so 'easy' is to encourage people to be indifferent about moral failure. But those who have been brought by the Holy Spirit to a true experience of repentance in this way could never think of it as a soft option or 'easy'. In some ways the hardest thing in the world is to say, 'I was wrong', human pride being what it is. And to be brought to our knees before God in true, heartfelt repentance is a costly and profound experience. Each time it happens we take another step forward on the road to holiness.

As Christians, then, we must expect that we shall sin and fail our Lord from time to time. When we do, we should not protest our innocence, nor weep for our shattered reputations. Instead, we should listen for the voice of God convicting us, and then agree with his verdict on our action. Confessing it and repenting it, we can then ask God's forgiveness for Christ's sake, and pray for his help to avoid the same sin in the future. After all, as Luther said, 'The truest repentance is to do it no more.'

Then, the sin repented and forgiven, we should put it behind us. God has forgotten it, set it an eternity away, so there is no reason for us to go on accusing ourselves over it. The healthiest and wisest thing to do is to follow Paul's example and 'forget what lies behind and strain forward to what lies ahead.'[2]

Failure—falling into sin, making mistakes—can be a great hindrance to our Christian growth; or else, wisely treated, it can be turned by God to our profit, so that we learn by our mistakes, and learn, too, how patient, understanding and realistic our God is.

Doubt

I remember preaching some years ago at a big church near London on the subject of 'doubt', and in the course of my sermon admitting that from time to time I was assailed with doubts about various aspects of the Christian faith. I expected a shocked reaction, but in fact afterwards a line formed at the door of devout church members who wanted to thank me for being frank about it. They had all been under the impression that they were the only Christians to have doubts, and had bottled them up guiltily for years.

In fact, any Christian who has never had a doubt has probably not thought very deeply about his faith. Doubt is part of faith—the other side of the coin. It can be brought about by circumstances, a shock, bereavement, depression; or by your own failure and sin; or by the failure of others; or by the onslaught of persuasive and clever unbelievers. Sometimes it is simply a failure, in a given situation, to exercise faith.

'Doubting Thomas' is the picture of all doubters. While remaining a disciple, he rejected a vital truth about Jesus Christ—that he had risen from the dead—simply because his own mind could not accept it and his own eyes had not seen it. Indeed, he demanded proof: 'Unless I see in his hands the print of the nails, and place my finger in the mark of the nails, and place my hand in his side, I will not believe.'[3] That is doubt carried almost to the point of obstinate refusal to believe!

It is worth noting that his doubts flowered when he was not with the other disciples. This is typical. Doubt flourishes in solitude. When doubts come, the best thing to do is to share them with other Christians; the worst thing to do is to keep them to ourselves, feeding them with our private fears and fancies.

But it is also worth noting how understanding and patient our Lord was with this aggressive doubter, Thomas. Proof was demanded—and that was precisely what was offered him. It would have been reasonable to expect Thomas to believe on the evidence of the other disciples (after all, it is on their evidence that we, today, believe in him). But Jesus Christ went all the way to meet the need of his baffled, cynical follower—and he still does. If our doubts are genuine, and we ask him to show us the answer, all the experience of Christians points to the belief that he will give us the evidence we need to cast out our doubts.

I recollect one night driving home from a youth meeting where I had been answering a barrage of questions from young people who were mostly sceptical about the Christian faith. I thought I had dealt pretty well with the whole range of objections—from Cain's wife to the problems of pain, hell, life after death and the rest. But suddenly, sitting in my car, I was engulfed with a wave of doubt such as I had never before experienced. For ten minutes or so I drove on with a sick feeling in my stomach, all my Christian defences gone, while my head reeled under the attack of the enemy. At last I screwed up what little faith I had left, and prayed, 'God if you're really there—before I go to bed tonight, answer this attack, prove to me that you exist and that I belong to you.' The attack subsided a bit, and I completed my journey home.

Before going to bed my wife and I usually read a passage of Scripture. At that time she chose what we read—not isolated passages, but consecutive readings through whole books of the Bible. My wife opened the Bible and began to read the passage which followed the previous night's reading—and it was the story of doubting Thomas. 'Do not be faithless, but believing. . . . Blessed are those who have not seen and yet believe.' She read—and my heart jumped! God had heard my despairing prayer, and had answered it in a way I could neither explain nor ignore. I am not suggesting that doubts are always answered in this very dramatic way, but I would argue that the prayer of the honest, doubting Christian is always answered somehow.

Is doubt a sin? Yes, but only if it is dwelt on, enjoyed, or made use of as an excuse for error, sin or compromise. Persistent doubt should be confessed and repented, certainly. But the real answer to doubt is faith, and faith is best nourished by dwelling, not on the mysteries and problems of Christianity, but upon Jesus Christ. If we get our minds off our doubts and on to him we should expect to see them fade away.

Discouragement

'We should never be discouraged,' says the old hymn. But the truth is that we often are. Circumstances most usually get us down—things not working out the way we expected, hopes being dashed, ambitions unfulfilled. And these things are also true for Christians.

It is dangerously easy to pin our hopes on other people—perhaps the ones who led us to Christ, or leaders in the church. If they let us down, or prove to be not as reliable or strong as we had hoped, then we get discouraged. Equally, we may get discouraged if our prayers are not answered in the way we expect, or if people we have hoped would turn to Christ reject our witness.

The thing to notice is how self-centred discouragement usually is. In every example I have given, it is *our* hopes, *our* prayers, *our* ambitions, *our* witness that is involved.

As in other realms, the answer is to divert our attention to Jesus Christ. It is utterly safe to pin our hopes on him. He is the one reliable friend we shall ever have. If we are trusting him, then we shall have confidence that the answer he gives to our prayers is the right one. Equally if we believe in the Holy Spirit we shall recognize that it is not 'our' witness that brings people to Christ, but his work. He is never a disappointment, and cannot possibly be. He is all we can ever need, and that should encourage us to 'never be disheartened.'

Fear

The world we live in is full of fears, some imaginary, many only too real. Over and over again our Lord's opening words to people he met on earth were, 'Don't be afraid.' But very often we are afraid, even when we have committed our lives to Christ, and fear can cripple our enthusiasm, blight every joy and cast dark shadows over every corner of life.

According to the Bible there is a right and a wrong sort of fear. In the New Testament, for instance, we are told to 'fear' God, to 'fear' the authorities and even to 'fear' those who are over us in the church.[4] On the other hand, we are not to fear anything that man can do.[5] We are not to fear man's scornful words.[6] We are not to fear for the future, or for things like wars and disasters.[7]

The right sort of 'fear' is really 'respect' or 'reverence', and that is a word we probably should explain. Many people associate it with ornate ritual or old-fashioned language—the etiquette, as it were, of religion. But in fact it goes much deeper than that. 'Reverence' is an attitude of mind, an attitude that puts God infinitely high and myself very low, that truly recognizes that when I come to him it is not a meeting of equals, but a subject coming to a King. When I have seen that God dwells in unapproachable light that no man has seen or can ever see, as full of holiness as he is of love, then I shall begin to grasp what 'reverence' is all about. To 'fear' God is simply to recognize him as God, and to approach him on those terms.

'Fear Him, ye saints,' says the hymn, 'and you will then have nothing else to fear.' The point is well made. If I 'fear' God, in a truly biblical way, then a million miles above everything else I shall want to please him. The scorn of men, the twists and turns of human history, death itself—these assume their correct proportions alongside the glory of the King of kings.

As with our other problems, the short answer to fear

is to turn our thoughts away from the objects of our fear and to fix them on the only One we should fear: our great God and Father. We do not fear him abjectly. He is no distant tyrant. But we see in him infinite power and wisdom and holiness, and the awe-inspiring 'otherness' of God; and our earthly fears assume earthly proportions.

However, having said that, one must add that there are other causes of fear which have little to do with our spiritual standing. If you find yourself seriously worried by irrational fears, that is, fears for which causes cannot be identified, then you should consult your doctor, who may well recommend psychological treatment. Often these fears arise from deep and subtle pressures and forces within us, and skilled help may be needed to bring them to the surface and remove them.

In the normal course of events, however, the problem is simply one of proportion. The head of the typing pool or the foreman or the college principal seem vast and dominating figures in our daily lives, and their words or opinions may carry a quite unreasonable weight with us. Our friends or relatives, or our colleagues, may also cause us to fear out of all proportion to their importance. Seeing God for who he is may help us to have a balanced view of people and events, not making us casual, or discourteous, but putting things into perspective. It is the same with events. It is possible to get unduly anxious over examinations, social occasions, interviews and so on. They can assume an importance out of all proportion to reality. Only a healthy, balanced view of life—as lived according to God's plan, to please him, to do his will—can deliver us from these sorts of fear.

Feelings

Feelings and emotions play an enormous part in all our lives, of course, and it is always dangerous to underestimate them. Love, joy, excitement make life what it is. In the Christian life emotion—the way we feel—has a vital role to play, but it can become exaggerated. When it does, the Christian life can become a terrible see-saw, with moments of dark depression and misery. This can lead to the all-too-common type of Christian who spends hours analyzing his own soul, explaining why he is 'up' or 'down' at any given moment, who lives on the kick he can get from big, exciting meetings, and collapses pitifully on Monday mornings.

How can the emotional element in faith become so exaggerated? It can begin from the very way we first hear the Christian message presented. Preachers and evangelists who stress *experience* rather than *truth*, who dwell at length on the dramatic changes Christ will make in our lives ('He'll put a smile on your face, a spring in your step'), are presenting their hearers with a totally misleading notion of what conversion really is. For many people the first emotional response to the gospel is one of acute tension, as problems hitherto ignored, or non-existent, begin to press in upon them. Christ gives us the resources to deal with them, of course; but to suggest, or even hint, that our problems will disappear, and that from now on life will be a serene, smooth joy-ride to heaven, is to court future emotional disaster. Paul's problems didn't disappear when he became a Christian, and neither will yours.

There is, it is true, often a 'honeymoon' period for the new Christian, when everything goes well and he (or she) experiences a wonderful sense of joy and relief.

If we assume that this is the normal emotional state of the Christian, however, we shall be ignoring half the New Testament. The Christian life is a battle;[8] there are serious and deadly enemies;[9] fears arise within us, and new pressures gather outside us;[10] temptations we never knew before will come, often in subtle and misleading forms, and we shall experience as never before the battle waged in the world and in our own personalities between the forces of good and the forces of evil.[11]

But the Christian does not despair. He knows that God will not permit him to be tempted beyond his endurance. He knows that the peace of God—which does not depend on circumstances, nor even on feelings—will guard his heart if he commits himself to God. He knows that, from the day he first received him, Jesus Christ himself, through the Holy Spirit, dwells within him, a constant and unchanging companion and friend.

Now some of us are more 'emotional' than others, and some will feel all these things more intensely than others. God comes to each individual in different ways, but he does not play games with us and his love never varies—there is with him 'no variation or shadow due to change.'[12] What we need to grasp is that the basis of our relationship with him is not *how we feel* but *what we are*—his children. God gave the right to all those who have received Christ to become his sons and daughters.[13] He does not go back on his word or vary his conditions. If you have come to him sincerely and without holding anything back, then his own word and promise must apply. You *are* his, and whether you *feel* his or not does not really matter.

There is a vivid example of this reliability of God in the face of our faithlessness, in Paul's second letter to

Timothy. There Paul writes:

The saying is sure:
If we have died with him, we shall also live with him;
If we endure, we shall also reign with him;
If we deny him, he also will deny us;
If we are faithless, he remains faithful—for he cannot deny himself.[14]

By the balance of the sentences–poetry, almost–and by the sense of the passage, the last line should have read:

'If we are faithless, he also will reject us.'

But in fact, that line differs from the others because it is not an 'also' line. Rather, it turns the whole arguement upside down! If we endure ... we reign. If we deny ... we shall be denied. But if we are faithless, it makes absolutely no difference to our standing, because our standing depends on God, not ourselves. A son is still a son, no matter how many doubts he may have about the family, or his own position in it. This is not an encouragement to be faithless, but a statement of fact about God. We come to him on the grounds of his promises, and they are dependable. Our feelings may go up and down, but that cannot affect anything as stable as the word of God.

It is very pleasant to have 'religious' feelings, and to be moved and excited by worship, by an eloquent sermon, by spiritual music or simply by the wonder of God and his world. If God gives you such moments of joy, thank him for them and treasure them; but do not presume that all the time and every day will be like that. When disappointments and discouragements come—when there are no wonderful meetings to go to, when you're cut off from other Christians, or when worship goes dry on you—turn again to God's wonderful promises in the Bible, claim their truth, and remind yourself that the Christian is a stable person because his life is built upon an unchanging God.

However, all that is not to say that we should disregard our feelings entirely, as often they can be a helpful guide to our inner situation. For instance, the Bible tells us that God will not hear our prayers if he sees sin in our hearts, unconfessed and therefore unforgiven.[15] So it may well be that if I find prayer dull and unsatisfying, or unreal, the reason for this lies in a sin I am refusing to recognize, repent or confess. In that case, my 'feelings' are a helpful guide to my true position.

Again, God intends us to have, as Christians, an inner serenity. This does not mean a permanent fixed grin on our faces, but a deep, underlying confidence in him. This peace 'arbitrates' in our hearts, Paul tells us.[16] That is to say, if it disappears God is warning us that something is wrong, perhaps in our attitude to him, or even in our attitude to another person. This wrong attitude has robbed us of our God-given peace. In this case, too, my 'feelings' are a helpful guide.

Thank God, then, for good and happy emotions. Bring to him, swiftly and openly, emotions of a negative or destructive kind. Do not expect a calm journey through life, but expect good company on the walk to help you overcome whatever crosses your path. Pray for, and expect to have, the inner serenity and balance of those who have committed their lives into the hands of God himself. Do not let your feelings dictate to you, but take sensible note of them in case the Holy Spirit is using them to say something to you—and especially to warn you of sin or spiritual danger.

WHAT IF I HAVE PROBLEMS?

[1] *I John 1.8–2.2*
[2] *Philipp. 3.13*
[3] *John 20.25*
[4] *I Pet. 2.17; Romans 13.3, 4; 2 Cor. 7.15*
[5] *Hebrews 13.6*
[6] *I Pet. 3.14*
[7] *Matthew 24.6*
[8] *I Tim. 6.12*
[9] *Ephesians 6.12*
[10] *2 Cor. 7.5*
[11] *Romans 7.23*
[12] *James 1.17*
[13] *John 1.12*
[14] *2 Tim. 2.11–13*
[15] *Psalm 66.18.*
[16] *Col. 3.15*

SELF-CHECK TEST 6

Circle the letter of the correct answer for each of the following. Choose the answer which most completely expresses the truth taught in the chapter.

1. Once a person is converted, problems, sins and failures
a. come to an automatic end.
b. slowly taper off.
c. may show up in new and disturbing ways.
d. are best ignored.

2. Sin assumes new dimensions in the experience of the believer because
a. conscience is made more tender by the Holy Spirit.
b. a counter attack is launched by Satan which, if successful, will permanently rob a Christian of his salvation.
c. Christians tend to sin more than non-Christians.
d. we have to get all the badness out of our systems by giving it free expression.

3. When a Christian realizes he has sinned he should
a. rationalize that he really hasn't sinned.
b. blame the old nature and leave it at that.
c. tell the Lord he is sorry and believe that takes care of it.
d. repent, confess and forsake his sin.

4. Doubts assail
a. all Christians.
b. only weak Christians.
c. only older Christians facing death.
d. only those who do not think very deeply about their faith.

5. Doubts
a. are always sinful.
b. tend to flourish in solitude.
c. have nothing in common with faith.
d. are best suppressed and ignored since this is God's way of dealing with them.

6. The best thing for Christians who are discouraged is to
a. focus their attention on some well-known, dynamic and successful Christian leader.
b. endeavour to change the circumstances which are causing the discouragement.
c. pray harder that their prayers be answered as they wish.
d. look to Jesus, the author and finisher of faith.

7. When facing the problem of fear in his life, the Christian should
a. never seek the help of a psychiatrist since this is unspiritual.
b. deny the reality of the fear since it is actually only an error of the mortal mind.
c. give God the proper place in his thinking.
d. determine to fear nothing and nobody.

8. In the Christian life there should be
a. an emphasis placed on truth rather than experience.
b. a deliberate suppression of emotion.
c. a complete absence of anything that might disturb our joy and peace.
d. experiences of elation and joy alternating with depression and difficulty.

9. In the balanced Christian life
a. feelings are the result of faith in the facts of salvation.
b. the facts of salvation are the result of faith in certain feelings.
c. faith results from feeling deeply enough about the facts of salvation.
d. salvation results from feeling deeply enough about one's faith.

ANSWER KEY

This answer key is designed to provide you with both the correct answer to each question and the number of the page where the question material is discussed. If you find your answer is incorrect refer to the page given for the correct answer.

chapter 1			chapter 2			chapter 3		
quest.	ans.	page	quest.	ans.	page	quest.	ans.	page
1	b		1	c	23	1	b	33
2	d	12	2	a	24	2	c	34
3	d	12	3	b	24	3	a	34
4	a	13	4	c	25	4	b	35
5	b	15	5	d	26	5	d	36
6	c	15	6	b	26	6	a	38
7	a	16	7	b	26	7	d	41
8	b	17	8	b	27	8	c	41
9	a	18	9	b	27	9	d	44
			10	d	28	10	c	45

chapter 4			chapter 5			chapter 6		
1	c	54	1	d	69	1	c	80
2	d	55	2	b	69	2	a	80
3	c	56	3	c	70	3	d	81
4	d	58	4	b	71	4	a	83
5	b	58	5	c	72	5	b	84
6	d	59	6	a	73	6	d	86
7	c	60	7	d	73	7	c	88
8	a	62	8	d	74	8	a	89
9	c	64	9	c	75	9	a	90
10	c	66	10	c	75			